The Nightowl's Dissection

The Nightowl's
Dissection
William Peskett

Secker & Warburg · London

First published in England 1975 by
Martin Secker & Warburg Limited
14 Carlisle Street, London W1V 6NN

Designed by Philip Mann

436 36709 2

The Random House Group Limited supports The Forest Stewardship
Council (FSC®), the leading international forest certification organisation.
Our books carrying the FSC label are printed on FSC® certified paper.
FSC is the only forest certification scheme endorsed by the leading
environmental organisations, including Greenpeace. Our
paper procurement policy can be found at
www.randomhouse.co.uk/environment

Printed and bound in Great Britain by Clays Ltd, St Ives PLC

London, Fakenham and Reading

For Naomi

Naomi looking at me,
she searches her repertoire
for a canvas fitting.
Sounding out my eyes
with thumbsmudges
on her palette's retina
she finds my true colour.

Naomi loving me,
she breathes organically
posing fixed and stained
under my giant observation.
Daring me on
to higher resolution
she takes my photograph.

Acknowledgements

Poems have appeared in *Broadsheet, Caret, Crabgrass, Eureka, Fuse, The Honest Ulsterman, The Irish Press, Lines Review, The London Magazine, Phoenix, Samphire, Soundings, Threshold, Transcript, Weyfarers;* and in *Poetry: Introduction II* published by Faber and Faber, *Cleaning Stables* pamphlet published by Ulsterman Publications.

Poems have also been broadcast in *Soundings, Words Alone, New Writing in Ireland* and *Moths and Mammoths* on BBC Radio 4, *Causeway* and *Young Poets on Stage* on BBC Radio 3.

Sandstones was published as a Posterpoem by the Arts Council of Northern Ireland with Charles Oakley as the Artist.

Contents

one

My Child

My child will have lungs
that are pink
like those of a lamb.
He will be smooth
and sovereign;
      will move
         like a tongue
as quick as his age.

My child will chase riverbirds.
Inside he'll be
flowing rapid like me.

My child, must it be you
who dissects the nightowl?
Its plumage
is darkly mysterious,
dropping silence on its prey.
My child, couldn't it be a dream?

Without a look behind,
my child
will slowly select a summer
and apply it firmly
to the spring.

Sandstones

I can find sandstones
and smell their decay;
can hear from birth
their granular murmur,
the cracking of cells.

I don't need your story
of the sinister sky.
It is all within me.
Death is my very last
hollow tooth.

I can pick up bones
and prod
the filigree disease
of their marrow
with quiet contortion.

The Question of Time

Where on earth
has the stumbling mammoth gone?
that giant tripper over nations
who used to think
the world was his
after the succulent brontosaurus.

The ages shed no tears for me.
I am not their resting
but their passing through,
left to watch
the intricate bees
in their noble art of dance.

Spider Birdfossil

I climbed the rock
and sat by the spider birdfossil,
set and split
by the mountainstress behind
and, as I watched the oldworld,
ages of volcanic valleys
eroded before my glacial stare.
And the   spiderbird flew
over carnal swamps,
it cried in flocks and tore meat,
not knowing of my flesh
but only its own flesh of stone.

Flying

Brooding over the recessions
of other lost planets,
the nightowl nestles
its last egg
as big as the sky.

Motherly, she fawns on us,
dropping down
breast-feathers from her flight.

The nightowl remains
unsnared, aloof, flying low
below the shoulder.

Guns

Everybody knows that guns were invented
by the Chinese,
that they're guaranteed not to explode unexpectedly
previous to depressing
that small lever below the barrel,
now called the trigger.

Everybody knows that you put in those bullet-
shaped objects
and that you point the open end
at the person you hate
and then how you sight down the barrel
and softly squeeze the trigger.

Everybody knows from the cowboy films
that there is a kick
and the bullet spurts away with an angelic report.
They know so well
how the person grunts and falls badly
to the ground.

But how many people
know that if you stick
the open end of the gun
into your mouth
and coyly pull the trigger
you hardly hear the bang at all?

You see your rich foaming blood,
spat on the floor, for a split-second.

Why I am the Last of the World's Great Lovers

When shadowboxing in the saturday backstalls
an extra feature sometimes flicks
across my mind.
It's a shame nobody seems to be wearing
clown lipstick anymore
or rolling soft make-eyes in silent scenes.
And nobody ever holds a girl
the way they used to.

Nobody does a silken swoon
across the railroad track anymore
or commits one of those flash
honkytonk suicides.

Everybody's forgotten that Valentino was once
the coming-soon at their local Odeon
and that his coffin was buried
in pink reincarnations and cards saying, come back, Valentino,
see you in Heaven.

One day I'll request his second showing
with dubbed stereophonic keyboards
and fill the kinema with my children
announcing,
by way of explanation, that this
perhaps is why I
am the last of the world's great lovers.

similie : you are

you are as infinite as the skyparabola
oh how
you drive me to simile out
of my head as smoky as a foxglove wing
out of my head you glide
as pacific as a treacle steamer
coasting on the empire line

On Your Pregnancy

Consider the heart:
feel it inside you
beating out
corpuscular crotchets.
Living blindly
it dispatches single
volumes of blood like ink,
urging your tissues
to describe the origins
of your individuality
in the air.

Consider our love:
can it be
that with one terrible
gesture I have entered
your blood's capacity
and spoken there
my brief autobiography?
I beware the hearts of men
that live faultless lives,
having peculiar pride
in my apprehension.

Consider the pain:
the poetry of our bodies
bore rhythm enough
unpublished,
yet your heart,
slyly blending us
in a new blood,
worked alone, privately
telling us nothing
of our secret intention
to start such mighty mechanism.

Consider the truth:
there is no reality
in creation, but beauty.
Not wishing to mix cells
we feared the beauty
myopically.
Now our individualities
are liquid loose
and your serum carries
nothing of me
save my sometime seed.

Window Dressing

The beautiful man and his wife
must have fled,
deserting their immaculate husks
like wholesome insects
on a jagged flight to a new life.

The copies that remain possess everything.
In their still and vigilant life
of display they need cocktail cabinets
and sofas
but have no inclination to move over,

to touch and merge.
The actual people, lush and naked,
are hovering on transient wings:
they're making love
out of hours.

On dark nights, through the window
on their brilliant home
I see them returning,
sheepish and ashamed,
slipping back into shape.

An Australian in Athens
(for Grant Newport)

More at home under the six dominions
of the Southern Cross
he travels,
applauding the black night,
to discover the dim disadvantage
of a Greek refinement.

A century of favour leaves no chance
for the Australian to gain.
Coming to Greece
only for his own praise
he stumbles through ruins
with a parched throat.

Thus, the breaker of wild horses
and wader of outback rapids,
the illumined sleeper-out
under stars
meets his maker,
says he's suspicious of the dark.

Impressionist Landscape

The mountains are mauve
and fishermen are scattered
paintbox remnants
from a primeval afternoon.

Birds hang in the sky
in an emulsion.
They knew more freedom
in the tethered womb-egg
of their primordial nest.

The sun is a canary smudge
on the brink of a molten lake
and the leaves on the trees
know nothing –
not even how to be leaves.

Crom — April 1969

the lake plane slices
the land from its reflection
like a fin

on a still day
there is twice as much of everything
except ripples

The Cottage

The journey,
the sense of driving through towns
like city folk
would make the cottage
stand in slightly foreign land.

Easing through the woods,
the smell of petrol,
the opening of doors
and we'd venture into damp air
to find week-old ashes
in every room.

Life would be slowly kindled.
In the day
old tracks would be tried,
old projects continued.
At night we could still see
the lough through the trees.

I could live for years
like that, let
all my aspects become
fresh and foliate,
let all my journeys
be to water's edge.

I hear the brambling woods
are being felled now,
old pathways torn
and badgers and squirrels
forced to uncustomary migration.

Soon the lough
will spill its secret
and its islands pave their shores.
The sound of motorboats
will travel far
over welcome water.

To the stranded cottage
it will make no sense:
to destroy its precious habit
makes a mockery
of weekends.

Explaining Snow to a Malay Boy

Snow conceals everything:
I tell him it's cold;
it's white,
it's like crushed ice from the freezer.
What else can I say?

I've seen snow deep as a rattan-chair,
I've seen it fall and lie
long into March.
The boy is lost in seasons
but what else can I say?

He's discovering a truth
about snow on his own —
that he'll never understand snow-reports,
never feel the cold
unless he wakes to find himself concealed.

Star and Sea

That star I now see
blended in the night's bright telegraph
has long since burnt out
and exploded.
The slowness of its fumes of light
across space provides
a second's vision of the past.
Gleeful time-traveller,
I forget I'm divided from a truth.

Cold water from the south
melts sombre
from the brilliant cap.
The slow currents north
take seven years to chill me,
to reach me with their dated clutter
from the ocean floor — time enough
for sea-change, a skin-change;
a new man reading old news.

two

The Nightowl

The nightowl preys
the breadth of the moon,
confronts the crossfire
between the men above
and the men below.

The nightowl escapes
to the dark side.
I will not pursue him
or bring him down to earth.
For me his secrets soar.

Cows

The cow is not a species
but a sex:
somewhere in a silver byre
the bull makes lonely love,
is emptied.

The farmer comes to the field,
conspires confinement
for the cows.
Moving in the herd
he finds suitable cradles
for unborn calves.

I wish I could comfort
these farmer's wives.
When I cross the field
they turn to watch.
They don't understand
when, deep and low,
I imitate their voice.

Whistling

The kettle is whistling,
hot water
is being digested
and vagrant steam is belched out
like a whistling
winter postman.

The kettle is whistling
and I wince
as I hold the scratching lobster
like an armlength trophy
and ignore the whistling
of its silent soul.

crayfish facts 1—4

i cant help but admire the crayfish
with its hide like crackling

its antennae are red like scalded
cocktail grasses

you couldnt pierce the crayfish
with a bowie spike

it lives in a beautiful fluid garden
its eyes are very small

ants

in the entrail arena
of tunnels
  a million ants
each with an arse as big
  as a bustle
each with jaws   grat-
              ing
like that penDULum blade
          pit
  their strength
against the cater-wrinkled
caterpillar
which has blindly stumbled

                            out of bounds

now
    just because they fuss
around the   alien
with such   Organised Efficiency
and just because they
    mes-mer-ise
  it with poison
and now just because they drag
its odd
      body   away
and rub their feelers at
Another Good Job Done
they think
they rule
     the world

Moths

Moths are hopeless in the air,
they are wild uncomfortable
companions to the wind,
enjoying the randomness of flight.

Moths have no face.
Smiling, I always think they
must drink light.
A cloud of them can absorb the moon.

The female moth is like the male.
When you crush it,
it doesn't bleed —
it sprinkles your hands with talcum.

Plants

Plants have the sexless advantage
of being silent.
They ignore the bees
which blunder like tactless cupids
from man to wife,
remaining haughty witnesses
to their own annual
pollination rigmarole.

There is no vegetable whisper
of endearment from their beds:
the plants part their petals
indifferently, quite aware
of their identical beauty.
Plants are mutely earnest, practical;
they communicate their love
by circumstance.

Moths and Mammoths
(for Trevor McMahon)

The moth swelters
through the night
composing dark shapes
as the sudden boundaries
to his hours.
His enemies will assist
his careful course
across the years.

The mammoth rips
delicate dreams
from ice-floes
waiting masterful
as they fall and melt.
Long-faced he stands,
the mountains walling in
his centuries of sight.

Taming Jackdaws
(for Mercy Hunter)

The black man has captured a jackdaw.
Tethering the bird to a chair
he cunningly plucks it
of its pin-feathers.
With a fast grin he dances aside —
the white man for his pleasure
will tame the bird. Revealing native wit
he'll make it imitate English,
train a nod and bow.

The house-guests, guarded,
see no need for taming
the quick-headed bird.
The white man losing interest, they think
it will die neglected on the chair
and that, in the end, the slick black man
might come to know the foible
of teaching birds to speak,
may cease to catch wild jackdaws,
taming only those already tied.

Frog's Flesh

Cold frog, my muscular little man,
white flesh smelling
good as chicken,
I know your flavour's more discrete.

Once I had you gingered:
repentent, I admit timidly tasting
your contract of duckweed
and spice.

Power, so neatly strapped
around your bones, when cooked
forms smooth packets,
relaxing in my mouth.

Pale frog, you lurch
through a world for cows and hens.
I ought to love you, little man;
your eye stays bright as leaf-dew.

Rainbow

Rainbow, you're a two-faced sort
of fellow,
you're a warped candybar
and the sun uses you
as a weapon against the shadow
of the rain.

Rainbow, you're not a self-made
chap at all,
you're just a compound of enemies
and the only reason
anybody likes you is because without you
they'd be nothing.

Looking at You

I can't see much in the sky.
The sun appears and lies to me,
telling me of weather.
It is too involved to be impartial,
I'll never believe
in its dull promise.
In league, the rain and sun
compare falsehoods.

Looking at you all
I know now your eyes
betray nothing.
Your clouds like crumpled poetry
in a way predict
the unlikelihood of rain.

Four Walls

you have four walls and a roof
   it's all you need
to contain your own atmosphere

your walls are stuck up
with etchings
      of Christ crucified
mezzotint choirboys
and
   weddingcake photographs
in paper frames
      but worst of all
  you have a second world war
    spitfire
whose propeller is built
      into your wall
to expel foreign bodies
  it's all you need
to contain your own atmosphere

The Inheritors
(for Paul Muldoon)

And the ones that got tough
ripped the soft parts
from the sea.
With a spine and a jaw
they pressed a clear advantage,
picking bones with ones
whose shadows met their own.
Gasping, they broke the surface.

The ones that had legs
came up where there was nothing.
Starting as one,
they split into bands
and savaged the green ground.
Ambivalent, they slid in the swamp
from home to home, cleverer,
keeping their options open.

The ones that could crawl
stood up and dried
the afterbirth from their backs.
Somehow they grew to break
the treaty of the land:
becoming gross they tore
the flesh of the sinless
and took three elements in their stride.

The ones that were feathered
came to know the slaughter
of the plain. Gliding from cliffs
they tumbled to the line of flight.
Innocent in the air, their shapes
against the sun began to drop —
below, their claws ripped fur
from nervous carcasses.

And the ones that gave suck
ran like warm blood
through high branches.
With a crib for their young
their lives might have been maternal
but for precedent. Not born
to run with the innocent,
inheritors, we kill.

The Nightowl's Examination

From a cloud of fledglings
one bird swoops
and becomes the nightowl.

After a million years
of knowing I impale him
on my skewer

and pluck his feathers
and cut him and
illuminate his dull organs.

I look into his head
and into its fine connections
with flesh and blood.

I take every cell from him
and every molecule
from each of these

and examine them.
I take everything. He gives
me nothing in return.

three

The Dissection

Laid bare,
the heartbeat continues.
Probing with opulent fingers
I try to reconcile the pieces
with the giblets of the table-bird.

Laid bare
by the plucking of feathers
my specimen takes the radial steel
like the spiking and piking
of a bull's withers.

Laid bare
is the mechanism of flight
and the breathly method of life.
Like a sky full of clouds
there is proud intention to fit.

Bottles in the Zoological Musuem

Bottles are for sleeping in —
they exorcise you
giving a live and pink
fluorescence to your skin.

Bottles contain you,
sinless and dreamless
you sink in their liquid
as eiderdown.

There are never men
in bottles — only animals
and babies and half-babies,
their softness gritting.

No man is accepted here.
I see a foetus crouch,
not in attack
but discovery of other shelves.

Dr Barker

Your mind plays no impatience
in science's symphony:
it explodes and blossoms
or recoils from other tunes.

You are playing
the dangerous game — microscopically
assessing your prospects
but logically choosing

through the riddle of the cell.
You'd laugh and say I held
the popular view,
that I couldn't see the medals

you're bound to be after.
I wish that I could sort
the notes so gently,
sifting the wealthy pages

for the key.
Leaving books, I'd pluck
a clatter of crescendo
for your ears.

Linnaeus

Linnaeus, you arranged the flowers
in binomial courtesies; you described
their dusty genitalia,
placing me between the beasts
and angels in your pornography.

I see now that you don't fit
in my lowly genus, you were chosen
to dispel mythologies,
to divide the Hydra
into falsehoods of weasel and snake.

Years before your time you found
holy order in the Arctic wastes.
Now you sit like a child
in your Lapland costume
beating your drum on the north wind.

Stem of Life

I don't want
to be told of my bones anymore
or shown
the painted cross-sectioned bowels
of my human body.
I don't want to know how my guts
or what my guts or why my guts.

I don't want to learn
of the minute stem of life
about which we still know nothing,
that stem of life
from seed of time
which binds with some reason the flesh
to the bone.

Dream

We have the episodes for a dream.
Firstly the birds:
waves of seagulls, forewarned,
billow out from the land.
The comfort is stealthily leached
from the rocks.

The canary in the gas-triggered cage
flutters. Next, far away we see
dark animals in stampede.
Our senses are dulled,
through disuse our powers
are shed.

To escape the dream
we see we must learn to run,
to stop, wide-eyed to graze,
to run,
to merge into our surroundings
to equilibrium.

Succession

No-one breathes
in this concrete-block village —
the pioneers have been routed.
Harassed, they spill over on to the land
leaving their neat compartments
to successions of skilled camp-followers.

Stopping in their steps to recover
they may hear on the quiet radio
of enemy advances.
Friends over the desert have succumbed.
If they rest too long without guard
they may drive themselves to drink.
Under pressure their organisation
is bound to decompose.

Eventually, the pioneers will surrender,
their tired bodies buried
in slow graves far over the prairie.
In the village, sand has covered
the allotments of their lives,
on the walls pale lichens grip.

If it had been said that their sons
knew nothing of the land
they'll have their day:
the concrete blocks will find
the way to fall.

Sandscape

Somewhere between the sea
and the tide's last lick
a woman lies,
too awkward to be sleeping.

Approach her like a bishop,
there is no need to hurry,
there is no blood —
the sea will never use
a murder weapon except
his own embrace.
Look, her face is white
as beeswax.

Her belly seems pregnant
and helpless as if her duty
were the sea's
vast procreation.

Do not touch her flesh,
it looks quite real
but splits like custard skin.
It is the reality
which makes you smooth her hair.

It is wrong to pity her,
look at her eyes.

Do not think of her as carrion
but stare into the sea
as she did,
drowning, living
all her life.

Birth and Death

Birth and death,
my strict parentheses,
like two old friends in a crowd
you are struggling,
tending to meet

and like two adjacent tyrant kings
you are threatening
my life's expansion
and filling my head
with only me.

Cleaning Stables

Years later I tried to clean out
his stable,
struggling to fork hard pellets
into a midden
the earth had almost swallowed.

Stupid from work
I became a pharaoh's slave —
in the dark
tall ducks and cats and sacred dogs appeared
to colour my portrait.

In knotted linen skirt I returned,
a shoveller of dung,
my complexion flat,
my home a menagerie of words
and sidelong glances.

The work-horse, long dead,
stood firm in his latrine.
I moved to pay him off, my currency
scarabs of jade.

Rock-Fall

I have tasted
the water now
and have hurried
through finger forests,
charred and alone.

I have breathed
the air and dug
the earth: have shuddered
the first stone blow
of rock-fall.

All I can do
is keep my mouth
well closed now
and my fluent fists
well hidden.

I can't be angry
with pebbles.
All I can do is wait
behind a now-still rock
and listen.

Standing in the Middle

Just as the slaughterer stands
in the shambles
of his own subdivision
so it is that my maker stands at the centre
while the universe revolves.

Neither sees at first
the significance of standing
in the middle: the butcher, reeling,
doesn't see that he's surrounded
by himself,

I don't recognise the way I started.
Spiralling inwards from the blood
to my destroyer I'll end.
I'll meet him like a man,
taking energy to unblind my eyes.

Colourblindness

Not seeing green
I blindly envy those
whose lives appear as mineral,
the colour of the soil.
I could fall as easily
into their situation
as on to the touch of grass.

The arbour of my life
has foiled my eyes for looking in,
letting me recognise foliage
only by shape. For the colour
there is purely no comparison.
Looking out, I learn to realise leaves
in terms of earth and stone.

Barman
(for my parents)

I'll return to the Black North
and tread lightly
where before I tried to dig my heels.
I've drunk good beer in Ireland
and have been weaned
and aged on the tightest wisdom,
the most serene observation.

I am a stranger in both lands,
am accepted wholly neither
in bar nor lounge.
I see how it is to blame
and be blamed
on both bleak sides
of the impossible water.

Where must I be born
to be loved by all my regulars?
How can I be the barman?
When up for the last round
what can they do
to see through the swing door,
the mirror in between.

William Peskett is the latest and youngest
arrival among a brilliant group of recent
poets in Northern Ireland. The intent
observation and delicate structure of his
poems are unusual. They feel their way
into situations with both tact and
exactness, and move with equal poise
through human relationships and the
natural world.
For the past few years, William Peskett's
work has been appearing in periodicals
and on the radio, and it attracted
special attention when a group of poems
appeared in Faber's *Poetry Introduction 2.*
The Nightowl's Dissection is his first
full-length book.

William Peskett was born in 1952 and
educated at the Royal Belfast Academical
Institution (he has lived in Northern
Ireland since 1959) and Christ's College,
Cambridge, where he read zoology.
Before university, he spent five months
teaching in Malaysia. He is married.